The BATHROOM LOL BOOK

———— • ————

COMMODIOUSLY COMPILED BY:
Jack Kreismer

HEAD WRITER:
Russ Edwards

RED-LETTER PRESS, INC.
Saddle River, New Jersey

ACKNOWLEDGMENTS

COVER:
Cliff Behum

TYPOGRAPHY:
Matt Taets

LAVATORIAL STAFF:
Jeff Kreismer
Kobus Reyneke
Lori Walsh

•

THE BATHROOM LOL BOOK

Revised and Updated 2011
Copyright ©2009 Red-Letter Press, Inc.
ISBN-10: 1-60387-115-2
ISBN-13: 978-1-60387-115-0

Red-Letter Press, Inc.
P.O. Box 393
Saddle River, NJ 07458

www.Red-LetterPress.com

The
BATHROOM
LOL BOOK

———— • ————

Mother-In-Law Jokes

They say that there are only three jokes in the world and that one of them is the "mother-in-law" joke- and that's not really funny. We'll let you be the judge...

Fred: "My dog bit my mother-in-law yesterday and I had to take him to the vet."
Frank: "To be put down?"
Fred: "No- to have his teeth sharpened."

•

Charlie took his wife and mother-in-law to the Holy Land and they were visiting Jerusalem when his mother-in-law dropped dead. He went to the American Consulate to make arrangements.

"Shipping a body back to the States is a very expensive business," the consul warned. "It can cost upwards of ten thousand dollars. But if you bury the body here it's only about three hundred."

"Hmm," Charlie rubbed his chin and thought for a moment, "No, I'm having her shipped home no matter how much it costs. Someone rose from the dead here once before and I'm just not willing to take that chance."

Now why does moisture ruin leather? Aren't cows outside a lot of the time? When it's raining, do cows go up to the farmhouse and say, "Let us in! We're wearing leather!"
—Jerry Seinfeld

A married couple were in a horrible accident where the wife's face was severely burned. The doctor told her that they couldn't graft skin from her body because she was too thin. The husband offered to donate some of his own skin and the doctor advised that it would have to come from his buttocks.

Arrangements were made for the operation, the surgery took place and the result was a resounding success. The wife looked as radiant as ever, her face not revealing one iota of the ordeal she'd experienced.

She was overcome with emotion and said to her husband, "Dear, I can't possibly thank you enough for the sacrifice you made."

"Honey," he answered, "I get all the thanks I need every time I see your mother kiss you on the cheek."

•

Wally took his mother-in-law by complete surprise when he presented her with a delicately scented, beautifully wrapped birthday gift. She unwrapped the present and opened the box to find a beautiful pair of earrings and a loaded handgun.

"Why, Wally, these are really gorgeous, but why the gun?"

"That's to pierce your ears with."

THOUGHTS OF THE THRONE

Running is an unnatural act, except from enemies or to the bathroom.

—**George Carlin**

He Said/She Said

He said: "Women should be obscene and not heard."
-Groucho Marx

She said: "Man invented language to satisfy his deep need to complain." -Lily Tomlin

•

He said: "Marriage is really tough because you have to deal with feelings and lawyers." -Richard Pryor

She said: "For marriage to be a success, every woman and every man should have her and his own bathroom. The end."
-Catherine Zeta-Jones

•

He said: "My wife has a slight impediment in her speech. Every now and then she stops to breathe." -Jimmy Durante

She said: "The only time a woman really succeeds in changing a man is when he is a baby." -Natalie Wood

•

He said: "I was married by a judge. I should have asked for a jury."
-Groucho Marx

She said: "Marriage is a relationship in which one person is always right, and the other is a husband." -Rita Rudner

---

The trouble with children is that they are not returnable.
—Quentin Crisp

True Tales of Clueless Crooks

Frank Margary was arguing with police as he was being held as a suspect in a store robbery. "There's no way the clerk can identify me," protested Margary. "I had my hat pulled down over my eyes."

•

A Hicksville, NY man was charged with petty larceny after a pet shop saleswoman heard chirping coming from his pants. When police arrived they discovered a pair of lovebirds in the man's pants. The suspect was promptly put behind bars. So were the lovebirds.

•

In retrospect, two Daytona Beach bank robbers probably wish they had gone over their plan better. As they say, the devil is in the details. The pair managed to get to the bank, even brandish guns and have the teller hand over the loot. After that their plan went awry. They jumped in their getaway car, hit the accelerator and immediately ran out of gas. The police were more than happy to provide roadside assistance.

•

Police had a warrant and were searching a house for a suspect. That's when the subject happened to show up. When questioned, he gave the police a phony name but didn't get away with it. Probably because he had his name tattooed on his face.

> *Have you seen the deer heads on the walls of bars, the ones wearing party hats, sunglasses and streamers? I feel sorry for them because obviously they were at a party having a good time.*
> —**Ellen DeGeneres**

Tampa police became suspicious after spotting three teenagers prowling around parked cars. They drove their unmarked car into a nearby parking lot and waited. Sure enough, the teens crept up to the car with the officers inside and went to work. That's when they learned a valuable lesson about grand theft auto: To wit- NEVER TRY TO STEAL A CAR WITH COPS INSIDE!

•

In Burlington, Ontario a man walked into a bank with a lit Molotov Cocktail and demanded money. When he hardly got enough to cover the gas in the bottle, he became very agitated and began shaking it violently. At that point, he went up in flames and ran out of the bank. Fortunately, the police were in hot pursuit. This was one crook who was happy to be taken to the cooler.

•

You've always heard that it takes money to make money. That apparently was true for a couple of New York bank robbers who couldn't afford decent transportation. Their junk heap getaway car had a "For Sale" notice in the window with their phone number written in large white letters which could be easily seen by one and all as they drove away. Hope they managed to unload the wreck because they won't be needing a car for the next five to ten years.

---

*You have a baby, you have to clean up your act. You can't come in drunk and go, "Hey, here's a little switch. Daddy's going to throw up on **you**."*
—**Robin Williams**

What's In a Name?

Arrested for public urination in Bowling Green, Ohio
- Joshua Pees

•

Arrested for possession of cocaine in Roseville, Michigan
- Denise Coke

•

Escaped from mental hospital in Warm Springs, Montana
- Terry Crazy

•

Charged with stealing toilet paper in Marshalltown, Iowa
- Suzanne Butts

•

Arrested for robbery in Ontario
- Emmanuel Innocent

•

Escaped from Canadian prison on three separate occasions
- Richard Slippery

By the time a man is wise enough to watch his step,
he's too old to go anywhere.
—Billy Crystal

Remembering Rodney

Say two words, "no respect", and you think of one comedian-Rodney Dangerfield. Now see if you can fill in two words to complete these one-liners from the king of self-deprecation.

1. What a childhood I had. Why, when I took my first step, my old man _ _ _ _ _ _ _ _ _.

2. I asked my old man if I could go ice-skating on the lake. He said, "Wait til it _ _ _ _ _ _ _ _ _ _."

3. I remember the time I was kidnapped and they sent back a piece of my finger to my father. He said he wanted _ _ _ _ _ _ _ _ _.

4. My uncle's dying wish was to have me sitting on his lap. He was in the _ _ _ _ _ _ _ _ _ _ _ _ _.

5. A hooker once told me she had _ _ _ _ _ _ _ _ _.

6. I met the surgeon general. He offered me _ _ _ _ _ _ _ _ _ _.

7. When I was born, the doctor took one look at my face, turned me over and said, "_ _ _ _, _ _ _ _ _!"

Life was a lot simpler back when boot up and log on was just something you did when you wanted to warm your foot by the fire.
—Red Green

Answers

1. tripped me
2. gets warmer
3. more proof
4. electric chair
5. a headache
6. a cigarette
7. "Look, twins!"

•

Once when I was lost I saw a policeman and asked him to help me find my parents. I said to him, "Do you think we'll ever find them?"

He said, "I don't know kid. There are so many places they can hide."

•

Q: What do you get when you cross Aretha Franklin with Rodney Dangerfield?

A: Someone who can spell R-E-S-P-E-C-T, but still doesn't get it.

THOUGHTS OF THE THRONE

I love it when my husband thinks I might leave him. He gets so insecure, he does the dishes. But I'd have to file for divorce papers to get him to clean the toilet.

—**Shirley Lipner**

GEORGE WASHINGTON AND THE CHERRY TREE:
THE MODERN DAY LEGEND

A father took his mischievous son to the Fourth of July company picnic. It was an honor to be invited and the boy promised to be on his best behavior.

On the long drive to the park, the father thought it would be a good, patriotic thing to tell his son of George Washington and the cherry tree.

As he related the tale of how little George Washington tried his new hatchet on his father's cherry tree and chopped it down, his father could see that he was very impressed. The boy's eyes widened even more when his dad told him how little George said, "I cannot tell a lie, it was I who chopped down the cherry tree," and was thus forgiven by his father for being so honest.

The pair arrived at the picnic but as the day wore on, the boy got antsy and set off looking for mischief. Sure enough, he found an opportunity when he noticed the porta-potties were all placed up on a hill with a sharp incline.

The boy picked one, gave a shove with his shoulder and it tumbled, end over end, down the hill and in the pond. Seeing that his prank had worked, the boy ran off into the woods and hid for a while.

One of the things that stays behind in childhood is baseball infield chatter. "Hey, batter, hey batter, batter...swing!" For instance, as an adult, I've never seen courtroom proceedings start with "Hey lawyer, hey lawyer, lawyer...sue!"
—Dobie Maxwell

Eventually the boy got hungry and decided to come back for something to eat. He no sooner returned than he was met by his father. "Someone pushed the outhouse down the hill," the father seethed. "Any idea who?"

The boy was scared but remembered his father's George Washington story and replied, "Father, I cannot tell a lie. It was I who pushed the outhouse down the hill."

With that, the boy's father gave him a good scolding in front of everybody at the picnic.

"But Dad," the boy protested, "What about the story about how George Washington's father didn't punish him for chopping down the cherry tree?"

"Well that may be," growled the father, "but George Washington's father wasn't in the tree when he did it."

•

"George Washington was walking down the street one day when they asked him for identification- so he pulled out a quarter."
-Steven Wright

—THOUGHTS OF THE THRONE—

My roommate is this completely psychotic, anal retentive nightmare roommate. He's the kind of guy who will eat bran on the toilet. He's insane. Why even eat the bran? Why don't you just buy the bran, throw it in your toilet and alleviate the middle man?

—**Lizz Winstead**

A Guy's Guide To Grilling

1. The woman goes shopping for the food.

2. The woman makes the salads, prepares the vegetables, and makes dessert.

3. The woman prepares the meat for cooking, places it on a tray along with the necessary cooking utensils and sauces, and takes it to the guy who is lounging beside the grill, beer in hand, trying to recover after singeing his eyebrows by using too much charcoal lighter starting the fire.

4. The guy places the meat on the grill.

5. The woman goes inside to get ice and drinks and more beer.

6. The guy takes the meat off the grill and hands it to the woman.

7. The woman gathers the plates, salad, bread, condiments, utensils, napkins, sauces and brings them to the table.

8. After eating, the woman clears the table and does the dishes.

9. Everyone praises the guy for his cooking and leaves.

10. The guy then asks the woman how she enjoyed her night off.

You tried your best and you failed miserably. The lesson is 'never try'.
—**Homer Simpson**

Actual Lines From College Admission Essays

- If there was a single word to describe me, that word would have to be "profectionist."

- I was abducted into the national honor society.

- I want to be bilingual in three or more languages.

- I have made the horror role every semester.

- I am thinking of possibly transferring to your college. I applied as an undergraduate but was weight listed.

- I first was exposed through a friend who attends Vassar.

- I would love to attend a college where the foundation was built upon women.

- My mother worked hard to provide me with whatever I needed in my life- a good home, a stale family and a wonderful education.

- Playing the saxophone lets me develop technique and skill which will help me in the future, since I would like to become a doctor.

- Such things as divorces, separations and annulments greatly reduce the need for adultery to be committed.

- Activities- Cook and serve homeless.

Flowers are one of the few things we buy, bring home, watch die, and we don't ask for our money back.
—George Carlin

DOCTOR, DOCTOR!

Patient: Doctor, doctor, I keep thinking I'm a laptop computer.

Doctor: You're just run down, let me give you some vitamins.

Patient: No, thanks. But I could do with some new batteries.

•

Patient: Doctor, Doctor, I need help.
Dentist: What's the problem?
Patient: I think I'm a moth.
Dentist: You don't need a dentist. You need a psychiatrist.
Patient: Yes, I know.
Dentist: So why did you come in here?
Patient: The light was on.

•

Patient: Every time I drink a cup of coffee, I get a stabbing pain in my left eye. What should I do, Doc?
Doctor: Take the spoon out of your cup.

•

Patient: I can't be cured? That's horrible! How much time do I have, Doc?

Health nuts are going to feel stupid some day, lying in hospitals dying of nothing.
—Redd Foxx

Doctor: Ten…
Patient: Ten years? Ten months? What?!?!
Doctor: Nine, eight…

•

Patient: You gotta help me, Doc. Every time I see a cat I sing "What's New Pussycat?" Last night I sang "Delilah" in my dreams. It's driving my wife crazy.
Doctor: You have symptoms of Tom Jones syndrome.
Patient: That's a new one on me. Is it common?
Doctor: It's not unusual.

•

Patient: Doc, Doc! I keep hearing a ringing sound!
Doctor: Try answering the phone.

•

Patient: Doc, Doc! I think I'm suffering from déjà vu!
Doctor: Didn't I see you yesterday?

•

"Doctors are crooks. Why do you think they wear gloves? Not for sanitary reasons - fingerprints." -Jackie Mason

You know there is a problem with the education system when you realize that out of the three R's, only one begins with R.
—Dennis Miller

Things You Don't Want to Hear at a Tattoo Parlor

"We're all out of red, so I used pink."

— • —

"There are 2 O's in Bob, right?"

— • —

"Gosh, I hate it when I get the hiccups."

— • —

"The flag's all done and, you know, the folds of
fat make a nice waving effect."

— • —

"Anything else you want to say?
You've got plenty of room back here."

— • —

"Eagle? I thought you said 'beagle.'"

THOUGHTS OF THE THRONE

*Maybe they should have a toilet paper museum. Would you
like that? So we can see all the toilet paper advancements
down through the ages. Toilet paper in the Crusades: The
development of the perforation. The first six-pack.*

—**Jerry Seinfeld**

Some Pretty Good Jokes

Three ladies of the evenings are brought before a judge.

"What do you do for a living?" he questions the first woman.

"Why, I'm a teacher," replies the prostitute.

"And what is your profession?" he asks the second.

"I'm also a teacher, your honor."

He turns to the last one and angrily says, "I suppose you're a teacher, too?"

"No, I'm a prostitute."

"And how is business?" asks the judge.

"Not very good," she answers, "there are too many teachers around."

•

Harry the handyman sounded the horn at the factory to signal the beginning and end of the work day. Every morning as he passed by the jewelers, he'd set his watch to the big clock in the store's window. One day his watch stopped, so after work he brought it into the jeweler for repair. When he picked it up the next morning, he

Now my credit cards pay each other. I've stepped out of the picture.
—Kelly Monteith

thanked the watchmaker for the repair work and also for the precise time kept on that clock in the window.

"Oh, think nothing of it," said the watchmaker. "I know it's always right. I set it every morning at the sound of the factory horn."

•

Two guys sat down for lunch in the office cafeteria.

"Hey, whatever happened to Harry in payroll?" one asked.

"He got this harebrained notion he was going to build a new kind of car," his co-worker replied.

"How was he going to do it?"

"He took an engine from a Toyota, tires from a Chevy, seats from a Hummer, hubcaps from a Caddy and, well, you get the idea."

"So what did he end up with?"

"Ten years in prison."

•

Two cowboys come upon an Indian lying on his stomach with his ear to the ground.

One of the cowboys stops and says to the other, "You see that Indian?"

My father would say things that make no sense like, "If I were the last person on earth, some moron would make a left in front of me."
—Louie Anderson

"Yeah," says the other cowboy.

"Look," says the first one, "he's listening to the ground. He can hear things for miles in any direction."

Just then the Indian looks up. "Covered wagon," he says, "about two miles away. Have two horses, one brown, one white. Man, woman, two children, household effects in wagon. Large dog in back, drooling."

"Incredible!" says the cowboy to his friend. "This Indian knows how far away they are, how many horses, what color they are, who's in the wagon, and what's in the wagon. Amazing!"

The Indian then says, "Ran over me about a half hour ago."

•

"Pardon me," a tourist says to a New Yorker, "Can you tell me where Rockefeller Center is?"

"This way," says the impatient New Yorker as he takes the visitor to the Empire State building. They go up to the observation deck and look out over the city.

"Look down there," the New Yorker says, pointing to the city streets. "Whaddya see?"

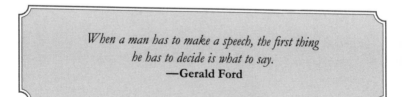

When a man has to make a speech, the first thing he has to decide is what to say.
—Gerald Ford

"Lots and lots of people," answers the tourist.

"And out of all them, you had to pick me?!"

•

A guy is standing on the curb, about to cross the road. As soon as he steps down onto the street, a car heads straight at him. He moves faster, but so does the vehicle. The guy thinks better of going across the street and moves quickly back, but the car changes lanes and is heading right for him. The guy freezes right in the middle of the road and the car comes screeching to a halt. The driver rolls down the window. Behind the wheel is a squirrel. "See," the squirrel says, "it's not as easy as it looks, is it?"

•

Gertrude's car was pelted in a driving hailstorm one night, resulting in hundreds of dents. The next day she visits a body shop to get it fixed. The repairman figures he'll have a little fun with her and tells Gertrude all she has to do is blow into the exhaust pipe really hard and the dents will pop out.

Gertrude goes home and blows furiously into the tailpipe. When her roommate asks what Gertrude's doing, she explains what the repairman advised her to do. "But it doesn't work," she says.

"Hellooo," says her roommate. "You gotta roll up the windows first."

People with honorary awards are looked upon with disfavor. Would you let an honorary mechanic fix your brand-new Mercedes?
—**Neil Simon**

O'Toole applied for a computer consultant's job at an Irish based company in Dublin. An American applied for the same position. They were given a test and both fellows did quite well, winding up with identical scores as each answered only one question incorrectly. The office manager thanked O'Toole for his interest but said that he'd be hiring the American.

"What?" squawked O'Toole. "I scored just as well and what's more, I'm Irish. Shouldn't the job go to the hometown boy?"

"We didn't make our decision based on your correct answers, but on the question you missed," said the manager.

"And why would that be the tie-breaker?" asked O'Toole.

"Simple. You both missed question nine. The American wrote down, 'I don't know,' and you put down, 'Neither do I.'"

•

Herb is telling Wally about the brand new thermos he brought along for their camping trip. "It's great," he said. "The guy at the store where I bought it told me it keeps hot things hot and cold things cold."

"Sweet," said Wally. "What do you have in it?"

"Three coffees and an ice cream sandwich."

I'm desperately trying to figure out why kamikaze pilots wore helmets.
—Dave Edison

A fellow walks into a bar wearing a really nifty shirt. "Where'd you get the neat shirt?" asks the bartender.

The man answers, "From Mike Ryan."

A second guy walks into the bar wearing some sporty pants. The bartender asks him, "Where'd you get those stylish pants, buddy?"

"Mike Ryan," he says.

A third guy walks in with a nifty pair of shoes. "Where'd you get those awesome shoes, pal?"

"Mike Ryan," he says.

All of the sudden, a fourth guy runs in naked and the bartender says, "Who the heck are you?"

"Mike Ryan."

•

An artist asked the gallery asked the owner if there had been any interest in his paintings. "Good news and bad news," said the owner. "A fellow asked about your work and wondered if it would appreciate in value after your death. When I assured him that it would, he bought all twelve of your paintings."

"Wonderful," said the artist. "What could the bad news possibly be?"

"He was your doctor."

I told the doctor I broke my leg in two places.
He told me to quit going to those places.
—Henny Youngman

In the locker room of a golf club, a cell phone sitting on the bench next to Harry started ringing. Harry picked it up and said, "Hello?"

"Darling," cooed a breathy voice at the other end. "I'm on Rodeo Drive and that mink I've had my eye on is on sale- only $25,000."

"Well I guess you should get it then," replied Harry.

"Oh, and while you're on the phone I wanted to ask you- the ash-tray in the Ferrari is full. Can I just get a new car?"

Harry shrugged and answered, "Sure."

"And the broker called me about that yacht. He needs to know if I want it. There's $750,000 in the checking account- just enough to cover it."

"Go ahead- live it up," replied Harry.

"Oh-thank you darling- you've been ever so generous," she said as she hung up.

Harry closed the phone, held it up in the air and called out, "Hey- Anyone around here lose a cell phone?"

•

NEWS FLUSH! Energizer Bunny Arrested: Charged With Battery

THOUGHTS OF THE THRONE

Life is like a movie- since there aren't any commercial breaks, you have to get up and go to the bathroom in the middle of it.

—**Garry Trudeau**

Bathroom Briefs #1

Just Don't Get Caught In the Rain

Ann Kagawa Lee, a designer in Honolulu, gave the world its first toilet paper wedding gown in 2009. Using origami and her skill for design, she created the dress not for blushing brides but for flushing ones. You only wear a wedding dress once and toilet paper was made for single use so why not combine them? The only problem is trying to keep grooms from squeezing the Charmin before the ceremony.

•

Flush With Evidence

A Jensen Beach, Florida, police officer was searching a suspect's home when nature called. This was one of those calls that you just had to answer- even in the line of police duty. The cop used the suspect's bathroom but when he tried to flush, the toilet wouldn't cooperate. Taking the top off the tank, there was a gun and several clips of ammunition stuffed down inside. The crook was arrested and probably charged with interfering with police business.

•

Counting Crow

Singer-songwriter Sheryl Crow wanted to bring attention to environmental causes by stating publicly, "I propose a limitation be

Monday is an awful way to spend 1/7 of your life.
—**Steven Wright**

put on how many squares of toilet paper can be used in any one sitting." She was joking of course but the idea gives a whole new meaning to the phrase "Three squares a day".

•

Just Dropping In

A woman in Russia was relaxing in her tub and had just dozed off when the apparently rotten timbers under her apartment floor suddenly gave way and the tub fell into the living room of the rather surprised couple below. The woman sustained only a minor injury. Perhaps her bubble bath acted as lots of tiny little airbags.

•

Fire Down Below

A Florida man was working on an old motorcycle, his pride and joy. He was revving it up on his back patio when suddenly it slipped into gear and crashed through the back door, dragging him along with it. It flew over on its side in the kitchen, spilling gas. His wife called an ambulance and he was taken to the hospital. His injuries relatively minor, he was sent home, but when he saw the state of his house and beloved motorcycle, he went into a deep depression. He sought the comfort and solace of the bathroom where he sat and had a cigarette. What he didn't realize was that his wife had sopped

---

I have a great dog. She's half Lab, half pit bull. A good combination. Sure, she might bite off my leg, but she'll bring it back to me.
— **Jimi Celeste**

up the gasoline with paper towels and threw them in the toilet. When he put the cigarette butt down between his legs to dispose of it, the toilet exploded. This time, the trip to the hospital wasn't so quick considering the damage to his nether regions. He did learn two valuable lessons that day; smoking cigarettes is dangerous to your health and the only butt that should be anywhere near your toilet is your own.

•

Case of the Pilfered Potty

Acton, Massachusetts, police responded to an oddball report and found that someone had indeed stolen a woman's entire bathroom. The toilet, sink, bathtub and fixtures were gone and the place was cleaned up. Investigation revealed that neighbors had seen a work truck with "Image Tile" parked outside. When they checked, it seems workers had gone to the wrong address and realized their mistake only after tearing out the bathroom, so they tidied up and left. The company offered the woman a new bathroom free of charge.

•

Question to ponder: If a mute kid swears does his mother wash his hands with soap?

THOUGHTS OF THE THRONE

Now what I don't get are these people who, instead of buying a four-pack or an eight-pack of toilet paper, they buy the single individual roll. Are you trying to quit?

—**Brian Kiley**

A Shaggy Dog Story

You know it. You've heard it. You may have told it- That extremely long-winded yarn with the pointless punch line. It's been around since way back when. When is that, you ask? Well, no one knows for sure but our dogged research has dug up what we believe to be the original shaggy dog joke. Here goes…

A wealthy English gentleman had his butler place full-page ads in newspapers all over the world, hoping to find his long lost, shaggy sheepdog. The finder's reward was a guarantee of a lifetime of luxury according to the dog-owner's plea. One morning over breakfast, a New York City fellow was reading the Times when he came across the advertisement. He didn't think much of it but later that day while strolling through Central Park, the fellow saw a stray sheepdog and recalled that it seemed to fit the description in the newspaper ad. The man left the park to buy a leash, returned and rounded up the pooch. The fellow bought a plane ticket for himself and the dog. They flew to London's Heathrow Airport and then hired a limo to escort them to the address cited in the advertisement. Once they arrived, the fellow rang the doorbell and the butler answered. He looked down at the dog and then said to the fellow, "Ah, yes. We're looking for a shaggy dog, but not so shaggy as that, sir!"

It's absolutely stupid that we live without an ozone layer. We have men, we've got rockets, we've got saran wrap – FIX IT!!!
—Lewis Black

Girl Talk

I'd much rather be a woman than a man. Women can cry, they can wear cute clothes, and they are the first to be rescued off of sinking ships.
- Gilda Radner

— • —

I think men who have a pierced ear are better prepared for marriage. They've experienced pain and bought jewelry.
-Rita Rudner

— • —

Marriage is very difficult. Marriage is like a five-thousand-piece jigsaw puzzle, all sky.
-Cathy Ladman

— • —

Why does a woman work ten years to change a man's habits and then complain that he's not the man she married?
-Barbra Streisand

— • —

After you've dated someone it should be legal to stamp them with what's wrong with them, so the next person doesn't have to start from scratch.
-Rita Rudner

The cat could very well be man's best friend but would never stoop to admitting it.
—Doug Larson

Marrying a man is like buying something you've been admiring for a long time in a shop window. You may love it when you get it home, but it doesn't always go with everything in the house.
-Jean Kerr

— • —

Behind every successful man is a surprised woman.
-Marion Pearson

— • —

When a man steals your wife there is no better revenge than to let him keep her.
-Sacha Guitry

— • —

Sometimes I wonder if men and women really suit each other. Perhaps they should live next door and just visit now and then.
-Katherine Hepburn

— • —

Men aren't attracted to me by my mind.
They're attracted to me by what I don't mind.
-Gypsy Rose Lee

I always remember the last words of my grandfather, who said,
"A truck!"
—Emo Philips

Going out with a jerky guy is kind of like having a piece of food caught in your teeth. All your friends notice it before you do.
-Livia Squires

— • —

A man on a date wonders if he'll get lucky. The woman already knows.
-Monica Piper

— • —

I've always said we got married because there was nothing on TV.
-Bette Midler

— • —

I'm going to marry again because I'm more mature now, and I need some kitchen stuff.
-Wendy Liebman

— • —

My ancestors wandered lost in the wilderness for 40 years because even in biblical times, men would not stop to ask for directions.
-Elayne Boosler

— • —

Kids are like husbands. They're fine as long as they're someone else's.
-Marsha Warfield

Start every day with a smile and get it over with.
—W.C. Fields

Grrroaners

Q: What do you call a dog that hears voices?
A: Shih-Tzu-Phrenic.

•

A man takes his Dachshund to the vet and says, "My dog is cross-eyed. Is there anything you can do for him?"

The vet says, "Well, let's have a look."

The vet picks the dog up and examines his eyes. Finally he says, "I'm going to have to put him down."

"What?" the man protested in horror. "Just because he's cross-eyed?"

"No," replied the vet, "because he's really, really heavy."

•

Q: What do you do with a broken dog?
A: Get him fixed.

•

Two hillbillies were having a conversation. The first hillbilly says, "You know, it's a dog-eat-dog world out there."

The second one says, "Yeah, but it could be worse. It could be the other way around."

They should put expiration dates on clothes so we would know when they go out of style.
—**Garry Shandling**

5 Silly Things To Say Today

1. Add "tra-la-la" to the end of every sentence you speak.

2. Refer to your friends in rhyming talk ("Molly Wolly" and "Tommy Wommy").

3. Answer every question with a question.

4. Write "I have laryngitis" on an index card and hold it up whenever someone talks to you.

5. A "Bathroom LOL Book" favorite, start singing in a public rest room stall and invite everyone to join in.

• • •

One (and only one) Knock-Knock Joke

Knock Knock.
Who's there?
Control freak... Now you say "Control freak who?"

THOUGHTS OF THE THRONE

I refuse to go to the bathroom on an airplane because if I'm gonna die in a cartwheeling ball of flames, it is not gonna be in a flying outhouse with my pants around my ankles.

—**Sabrina Matthews**

Hilarious Headlines

The massive effect of our economy woes and resulting employee cutbacks has apparently taken its toll on proofreaders as these headlines indicate.

Legislator Wants Tougher Death Penalty

— • —

Marijuana Issue Sent To A Joint Committee

— • —

World Bank Says Poor Need More Money

— • —

Fire Officials Grilled Over Kerosene Heaters

— • —

Federal Agents Raid Gun Shop, Find Guns

— • —

Police: Crack Found in Man's Buttocks

— • —

Stolen Painting Found by Tree

I never loved anyone so much at first meeting. But let's make no mistake why these babies come here: To replace us. We'll see who's wearing the diapers when all this is over.
—Jerry Seinfeld

Got Milk?

Q: What do you call a cow with no legs?
A: Ground beef.

•

There was a fly buzzing around the cow's ear while the farmer was milking it. Next thing you know, the fly was in the bucket of milk—in one ear, and out the udder.

•

Q: What do you get from a pampered cow?
A: Spoiled milk.

•

A couple of cows were chatting while grazing when one says to the other, "Hey, have you heard about that mad cow disease that's going around?"

"Yeah. It makes me glad I'm a penguin."

•

Q: What do you call a cow that's just had a baby?
A: De-calfinated.

My dad's pants kept creeping up on him. By sixty-five he was just a pair of pants and a head.
—Jeff Altman

Three pigs are in the barnyard. The first one says,
"Oink, oink."
The second pig says, "Oink, oink, oink."
The third pig says, "Moooo."
The other two pigs do a double take.
Overhearing the third pig, the farmer asks, "What did you say?"
"Mooooooo."
"That's crazy," says the farmer. "Pigs don't say 'moooo'!"
"I know, but I'm trying to learn a second language."

• • •

Pick Up Put Downs

Guy: Haven't I seen you someplace before?
Gal: Yeah, that's why I don't go there anymore.

•

Guy: I'd like to call you. What's your number?
Gal: It's in the phone book.
Guy: But I don't know your name.
Gal: That's in the phone book too.

Some people think my friend George is weird because he has false teeth. I think George is weird because he has false teeth with braces on them.
—Steven Wright

Guy: Is this seat empty?
Gal: Yes, and this one will be too if you sit down.

•

Guy: Your place or mine?
Gal: Both. You go to yours and I'll go to mine.

•

Guy: So what do you do for a living?
Gal: I'm a female impersonator.

•

Guy: Hey baby, what's your sign?
Gal: Do Not Enter.

•

Guy: Hey sugar lips, I really know how to please a lady.
Gal: Then why aren't you leaving me alone?

•

Guy: I would go to the end of the world for you.
Gal: Great! And do you think you could stay there?

THOUGHTS OF THE THRONE

I don't know if I want a fuzzy cover on my toilet seat, but I want to meet whoever invented them. Who lifted a toilet seat and thought, "That needs a hat."

—Rita Rudner

A Phone Line They Probably
Shouldn't Automate... 1-800-THERAPY

Hello, Welcome to the Psychiatric Hotline.

If you are obsessive-compulsive, please press 1 -repeatedly.

If you are co-dependent, please ask someone to press 2.

If you have multiple personalities, please press 3, 4, 5 and 6.

If you are paranoid-delusional, we know who you are and what you want. Just stay on the line so we can trace the call. The black helicopter will arrive shortly.

If you are schizophrenic, listen carefully and a little voice will tell you which number to press.

If you are delusional, press 7 and your call will be transferred to the mother ship.

If you have amnesia, press 8 and state your name, address, phone, date of birth, social security number and your mother's maiden name.

If you have short-term memory loss, press 9. If you have short-term memory loss, press 9. If you have short-term memory loss, press 9. If you have short-term memory loss, press 9.

If you have abandonment issues, please hold on the line. Someone will be (click...dial tone).

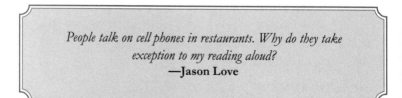

People talk on cell phones in restaurants. Why do they take exception to my reading aloud?
—Jason Love

Heavenly Humor

A guy goes to confession. He says, "Father, forgive me, for I have sinned. I was skiing when I saw my boss on the same slope. He didn't recognize me because I was wearing my ski mask so I skied over to where he was, pushed him and roared with laughter as he rolled over and over down the hill."

"Why are you telling me this again?" asks the priest. "That's the fifth time you've confessed this transgression."

The guy answers, "I know. I just like talking about it."

•

A lawyer is greeted by St. Peter at the Pearly Gates.

"St. Peter, this must be a mistake," says the lawyer. "I can't be dead yet. I was in my office working on a real important case... so important it might make me a partner in the law firm. I was just sitting at my desk. I wasn't sick. I didn't have a heart attack. Now all of a sudden I'm here. What's the story?"

St. Peter asks the lawyer his name, then goes over to his computer and enters it. After a few moments, St. Peter says, "Well, the computer says you died of old age."

On my sixteenth birthday my parents tried to surprise me with a car, but they missed.
—**Tom Cotter**

"What!?!" exclaims the lawyer. "I'm only 32 years old!"

St. Peter looks at the screen again and then says, "Hmmm… That's strange. It says here that, according to your billable hours, you're 103."

•

Q: What branch of the government does St. Peter work for?
A: The Eternal Revenue Service.

•

They say that Noah would have made a great businessman. After all, he managed to float a company when the whole world was in liquidation.

•

Q: How was the Lord able to create the world in six days?
A: He didn't have to provide any documentation.

•

Riley: I sometimes wonder what our ancestors would think of our country today.
Fenster: Well, when I get to heaven, I'll ask them.
Riley: What if they didn't go to heaven?
Fenster: Then you can ask them.

I'm on that diet where you eat vegetables and drink wine. That's a good diet. I lost ten pounds and my driver's license.
—Larry The Cable Guy

A small plane is flying with four people aboard: the pilot, a priest, a world-famous scientist and a drifter. The pilot announces that the plane is in deep trouble and they must flee for safety. "Unfortunately we only have three parachutes for the four of us," says the pilot.

The scientist immediately exclaims, "I am the smartest man in the world. I must be saved." He grabs the parachute and jumps from the plane.

The priest volunteers, "I've lived for a long time. The Lord awaits me. You two may take the remaining parachutes."

The drifter says, "Don't worry, Father. We've got one for you. The smartest man in the world just parachuted with my knapsack."

•

Lil' Matt was kneeling beside his bed, saying his prayers. His mother said, "Matty, I can't hear you."

Lil' Matt replied, "I wasn't talking to you."

•

Q: Where is insurance mentioned in "the Bible"?
A: When David gave Goliath a piece of the rock.

Guys are like dogs. They keep comin' back. Ladies are like cats. Yell at a cat one time, they're gone.
—Lenny Bruce

Laughable Laws

Ours is a society of law and the more laws there are, the better off society is. At least that seems to be the viewpoint of many of our loony legislators.

In Alabama, if you play dominoes on Sunday, the long arm of the law just might reach out and knock them all over. Must be tough to be in jail after being arrested for this. "What you in for?" "Armed robbery... You?" "Dominoes."

•

Alabama's even tougher on a-salt cases where it's possible to get the death penalty for putting salt on railroad tracks. Seems it would be far worse to sprinkle pepper on the tracks because then you'd get A-CHOO! choo train.

•

Up in Fairbanks, AK, should you give alcohol to a moose, you just may end up in the cooler yourself. So if you see a flying squirrel carrying a six-pack you better warn him. Nobody likes a boozy Bullwinkle.

•

In Minnesota, it's illegal to tease skunks. Also very stupid!

In schools, you can always identify the children who were dressed by their fathers. Such children should have signs pinned to their strange attire that say, "Please do not scorn or mock me. I was dressed by my father, who sees colors the way Beethoven heard notes."
—**Bill Cosby**

Florida frowns on unmarried women who parachute on Sunday. So this warning to the Sunshine State Skydiving Sisterhood – jump out of a plane and you'll land in jail!

•

In South Bend, Indiana, they've outlawed monkeys smoking cigarettes. Apparently this was once quite a problem. They would have tried a stop-smoking program but the monkeys complained that the nicotine patches kept pulling their hair out.

•

Not much is illegal in Nevada but apparently they do take issue with riding a camel on the highway. It seems they don't approve of a vehicle that carries its own speed bumps.

•

New Jersey, home to many of the nuttiest laws in the land, also provides us with one of the most famous. In Trenton, it is against the law to throw a bad pickle into the street. You might say it's dill-legal.

•

In Wichita, it is illegal to carry a concealed bean snapper. Guess they had a string of these crimes.

Someone asked me, "What's your idea of a good time?" I said, "6:45."
—Dick Cavett

Courtroom Comedy

The following are authentic questions asked by attorneys during trials.

"You were there until the time you left, is that true?"

— • —

"The youngest son, the twenty-year old, how old is he?"

— • —

"Were you present when your picture was taken?"

— • —

"Were you alone or by yourself?"

— • —

"Was it you or your younger brother who was killed in the war?"

— • —

"Did he kill you?"

— • —

"How far apart were the vehicles at the time of the collision?"

— • —

"How many times have you committed suicide?"

If Kobe Bryant had a kidney stone, would he pass it?
—Jay Leno

Trial Talk

We can't make this stuff up, folks

Defendant: Judge, I want you to appoint me another lawyer.
Judge: And why is that?
Defendant: Because the Public Defender isn't interested in my case.
Judge (to Public Defender): Do you have any comments on the defendant's motion?
Public Defender: I'm sorry, your Honor. I wasn't listening.

•

Judge: I know you, don't I?
Defendant: Uh, yes.
Judge: All right, tell me, how do I know you?
Defendant: Judge, do I have to tell you?
Judge: Of course, you might be obstructing justice not to tell me.
Defendant: Okay. I was your bookie.

•

From a defendant representing himself...
Defendant: Did you get a good look at me when I stole your purse?
Victim: Yes, I saw you clearly. You are the one who stole my purse.
Defendant: I should have shot you while I had the chance.

The trouble with the average family is it has too much month left over at the end of the money.
—Bill Vaughan

Things You Don't Want To Hear In Surgery

"What's this doing here?"

— • —

"Someone call the janitor - we're going to need a mop."

— • —

"Wait a minute! If this is his spleen, then what's that?"

— • —

"Hand me that....uh....that uh....thingie."

— • —

"Everybody stand back! I lost my contact lens!"

— • —

A couple having trouble making babies go to see a doctor. The doctor gives the husband a revolutionary new injection made from monkey glands. Exactly nine months later his wife has a baby. When the nurse comes out of the delivery room with the news, the husband excitedly asks, "Is it a boy or a girl?"

The nurse responds, "We won't know until it comes down off the light fixtures."

THOUGHTS OF THE THRONE

I've learned that life is like a roll of toilet paper; the closer you get to the end, the faster it goes.

—Andy Rooney

Lavatory Label A Wacky Winner

The winner of the 2009 Wacky Warning Label Award goes to the Original Off-Road Commode, a toilet seat that attaches to a trailer hitch. It was designed for sportsmen on the go but apparently the manufacturer was afraid someone would utilize it while the vehicle was in motion so they included the warning "Not for use on moving vehicles". It's a pity- think how that would have discouraged tailgating.

The outfit that sponsors this zany contest has been uncovering loony labels since before the start of the century. Following is a random collection:

Cannot be made non-poisonous.
Windshield Washer Fluid

— • —

Caution: Do not use this hammer to strike any solid object.
Hammer

— • —

Caution: Never drive with the cover on your windshield.
Automobile Windshield Cover

Last week, my aunt passed away. She was cremated.
We think that's what did it.
—Jonathan Katz

Directions: Use like regular soap.
Dial Soap

— • —

Do not attempt to stop chain with your hands or genitals.
Swedish Chain Saw

— • —

Do not drive car or operate machinery.
Children's cough medicine

— • —

Do not eat toner.
Laser Printer Cartridge

— • —

Do not turn upside down. (printed on bottom of the box)
Tesco's Tiramisu dessert

— • —

Do not use for drying pets.
Microwave Oven

— • —

I used to be a heavy gambler. Now I just make mental bets.
That's how I lost my mind.
—**Steve Allen**

Warning: Not for use as earplugs.
Silly Putty

For external use only!
Curling Iron

— • —

For indoor or outdoor use only.
Christmas lights

— • —

Do not eat urinal cakes.
Rest Stop in Wisconsin

— • —

Not dishwasher safe.
TV Remote Control

— • —

Open packet and eat contents.
Pack of Peanuts

— • —

THOUGHTS OF THE THRONE

Why do they call it the restroom? Is there anybody just resting in this room?

—**Dane Cook**

The Quayle Awards

Dedicated to those who have put their foot in their mouth all the way up to their knee

"I'll tell you it's big business. If there is one word to describe Atlantic City, it's big business. Or two words- big business."
-Donald Trump

— • —

"I've never really wanted to go to Japan. Simply because I don't like eating fish. And I know that's very popular out there in Africa."
-Britney Spears

— • —

"We have a lot of kids who don't know what work means. They think work is a four-letter word."
-Sen. Hillary Clinton

— • —

"A teacher asked us if anybody knew the names of the continents. I was sooo excited. I was like, 'Damn it! It's my first day of 7th grade, I'm in junior high and I know this answer.' So I raised my hand, I was the first one, and I said 'A-E-I-O-U!'"
-Jessica Simpson

I think Pringles' original intention was to make tennis balls. But the day the rubber was supposed to show up they got a big load of potatoes instead.
—Mitch Hedberg

Little Johnny Jokes

Little Johnny went into a supermarket, picked out a big box of laundry detergent and went to the checkout. The grocer asked Johnny if he had a lot of laundry to do. "Nah," said Johnny, "I'm gonna wash my dog."

"You shouldn't wash him with this," said the grocer. "It's real strong stuff and could make him sick or even worse."

But Johnny insisted on buying the suds. A few days later, he went back to the store to buy some candy. The grocer asked him how the dog was doing. Johnny said, "Oh, he died."

The grocer said he was sorry to hear that but repeated that he was afraid the detergent would be extremely harmful to the dog. Johnny said, "I don't think it was the detergent that did him in." The grocer asked, "What was it then?"

"I think it was the spin cycle."

•

The teacher asks Little Johnny if he knows his numbers. He says, "Yes. My father taught me."

"Good. Then what comes after four?"

The trouble with unemployment is that the minute you wake up in the morning you're on the job.
—Slappy White

"Five," answers Johnny.

"What comes after eight?"

"Nine," says Johnny.

"Excellent," says the teacher. "Sounds like your dad taught you well. And what comes after ten?"

"A Jack."

•

Little Johnny asks his mother her age.

She replies, "Gentlemen don't ask a lady how old she is."

Johnny then asks his mother how much she weighs. His mother once again answers, "Gentlemen don't ask ladies that question."

Johnny then asks, "Why did Daddy leave you?"

His mother says, "You shouldn't ask that."

A bit later, Johnny gets into some mischief. Rummaging through his mother's purse, he comes across her driver's license. He runs up to his mother and excitedly says, "I know all about you now. You're 35 years old, you weigh 125 pounds and Daddy left you because you got an 'F' in sex!"

If you don't know where you're going, you could wind up someplace else.
—Yogi Berra

As a spelling lesson, Mrs. Jones asked her students to volunteer what their parents did for a living and then to spell out that occupation.

The first student raised her hand and Mrs. Jones said, "Yes, Mary?"

Mary answered, "My father is a banker- B-A-N-K-E-R. And if he was here today, he would give us all a shiny new penny."

Then Jimmy raised his hand. When Mrs. Jones called on him, he said, "My father is a baker- B-A-K-E-R. If he was here today, he would give us all a cookie."

"Very good," the teacher said.

Tommy was next and he announced, "My father is an accountant. A-K, no wait, A-C-K, no..."

The teacher gently cut him off and told him to sit back down and to think about it for a while. When he thought he knew how to spell it, he could try again.

Little Johnny then raised his hand in excitement. Mrs. Jones said, "Yes, Johnny."

Johnny said, "My father is a bookie- B-O-O-K-I-E. And if he was here today, he would give us all 10 to 1 odds that Tommy will never be able to spell 'accountant.'"

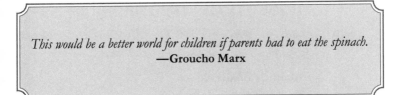

This would be a better world for children if parents had to eat the spinach.
—Groucho Marx

"Do you know about the birds and the bees?" asks Little Johnny's father.

"I don't want to know!" Little Johnny says, bursting into tears.

Johnny's father is perplexed and asks him what's wrong.

Little Johnny sobs, "First, there was no Santa Claus, then no Easter Bunny, and then no Tooth Fairy. If you're gonna tell me that grownups don't really have sex, I've got nothing left to believe in."

•

The teacher scolded Little Johnny. "This essay you've written about your pet dog is exactly the same as the one your brother wrote."

"Of course it is," explained Johnny. "It's the same dog!"

•

The class was instructed to write an essay on what they would do if they had a million dollars.

Little Johnny handed in a sheet of blank paper.

The teacher said: "Johnny, you've done nothing. Why?"

"Because that's exactly what I'd do if I had a million dollars."

THOUGHTS OF THE THRONE

I walk into rooms and I don't know why I'm there. I'm like, 'Why am I standing in front of the toilet now?'

—**Matthew Broderick**

Little Johnny: I ate a submarine sandwich for lunch and I think I'm going to be sick.
Johnny's Mother: What makes you say that?
Little Johnny: It's starting to surface.

•

On the first day of school, around the time of the mid-morning break, the kindergarten teacher said, "If anyone has to go to the bathroom, hold up two fingers."

From the back of the room Little Johnny hollered, "How will that help?"

•

The class was assigned to write about something unusual that happened.

When Little Johnny was called on, he got up and began to read, "Dad fell in the well last week…"

"My gosh!" interrupted his teacher. "Is he okay?"

"He must be," said Johnny. "He stopped calling for help yesterday."

Latinos outnumber black people now. I'm not too happy about it. It's only a matter of time before we lose our month. Soon as they figure it out they're gonna have Latino History Month, and all we'll have left is Cinco de Negro.
—Alonzo Bodden

One Sunday morning in church, Little Johnny said, "Mommy, I gotta pee."

His mother said, "It's not polite to say the word 'pee' in church. From now on, if you have to pee, just say that you have to 'whisper.'"

The next week, Johnny was in church with his father when he said, "Daddy, I have to whisper."

His dad said, "Okay, just whisper in my ear."

•

Little Johnny's neighbors had a baby that was born with no ears. When the parents invited Little Johnny's family to come over and see their new baby, his parents were afraid that their son would make a wise crack. Little Johnny's dad decided it would be best to have a talk with him beforehand.

He said, "Johnny, you're not to say one word about the baby not having any ears or I'll take your Wii away."

"I promise I won't say anything," said Little Johnny.

Once at the neighbors, Little Johnny leaned over the baby's crib, then looked at the baby's mother and said, "You have a beautiful little baby."

Man is the only animal, I believe, who pretends he is thinking of other things while he is eating.
—Robert Lynd

The mother said, "Well, thank you very much, Johnny."

Johnny continued, "He has perfect little hands and perfect little feet. And look at his pretty little eyes. Did his doctor say that he can see good?"

The baby's mother responded, "Why yes, Johnny... his doctor said he has 20/20 vision."

Little Johnny said, "Well, it's a good thing, 'cuz he couldn't wear any glasses!"

•

Dinkins had been pounding the pavement all day. The life of a door-to-door salesman can be hard. On his first call after lunch, he rang the doorbell of an imposing home in a wealthy neighborhood. As the door opened, he saw Little Johnny standing there smoking a cigar and drinking a bourbon. Over his shoulder, Dinkins could see the living room smeared with chocolate.

"Is your mother home?" Dinkins asked.

Little Johnny took a puff of his cigar and replied, "What do you think?"

My entire childhood we had the letters m-a-l-e painted on the side of the mailbox. By the time I was in eleventh grade, I was like, "That ain't right. That M is supposed to be capitalized, isn't it?"
—Jeff Foxworthy

Cosmic Questions

Does Italy's Tower of Pisa look straight to a leaning tourist?

— • —

How do you draw a blank?

— • —

If love is blind why is lingerie so popular?

— • —

How do you throw away a garbage can?

— • —

If a tortoise loses his shell, is it homeless?

— • —

Do vegetarians eat animal crackers?

— • —

Is half of a large intestine a semi-colon?

— • —

Would the ocean be deeper without sponges?

Now I know what a statesman is; he's a dead politician.
We need more statesmen.
—**Bill Vaughan**

If you locked a humidifier and a de-humidifier in a room who would win?

— • —

If you get cheated by the Better Business Bureau, who do you complain to?

— • —

What if the Hokey Pokey *is* what it's all about?

— • —

Whatever happened to the first 6 "Ups"?

— • —

Ever wonder what happened to Preparations A through G?

— • —

What do you pack styrofoam in?

THOUGHTS OF THE THRONE

Q: *If there's H2O on the inside of a fire hydrant, what's on the outside?*

A: *K9P.*

Definitions by Gender

Thingy
Female: Any part under a car's hood.
Male: The strap fastener on a woman's bra.

•

Vulnerable
Female: Fully opening up one's self emotionally to another.
Male: Playing football without a helmet.

•

Communication
Female: The open sharing of thoughts and feelings with one's partner.
Male: Scratching out a note before suddenly taking off for a weekend with the boys.

•

Laundry
Female: An assemblage of clothes ready for the washing machine.
Male: After all drawers have been searched, an emergency reserve of clothes where one might find something that smells slightly less than what you have on.

Instead of getting married again, I'm going to find a woman I don't like and just give her a house.
—Rod Stewart

Butt
Female: The body part that every item of clothing manufactured makes "look bigger."
Male: What you slap when someone's scored a touchdown, homered, or sunk a three-pointer. Also comes in handy for mooning.

•

Commitment
Female: A desire to get married and raise a family.
Male: Not trying to pick up other women while out with one's girlfriend.

•

Space
Female: A useful quality of one's dwelling which allows for both storage and ease of decoration.
Male: Where Han Solo and Captain Kirk work.

•

Entertainment
Female: A good movie, concert, play or book.
Male: Anything that can be done while drinking.

My wife told me to take out the garbage. I told her,
"You cooked it; you take it out."
—Rodney Dangerfield

Top Ten Signs You're Addicted to Your Cell Phone

10. Parts of your body actually tingle when you get free cell phone minutes.

9. Raising your children interferes with programming your speed dial.

8. Formal dress means matching your outfit to your cell phone cover.

7. When you are in a car accident, your first response is, "Can you hold on a sec? I'm hemorrhaging."

6. You use the menu light as your night light.

5. Those huge bulging biceps on your thumbs.

4. You send periodic text messages to yourself just to make sure the phone is still working.

3. Your retirement plan is based on saving up all your rollover minutes.

2. You're the one that the "Can you hear me now?" guy is always talking to.

And the Number One Sign That You're Addicted to Your Cell Phone....

1. Your most satisfying intimate relationship is between you and your cell phone vibrating in your pocket.

THOUGHTS OF THE THRONE

Getting married's a lot like getting into a tub of hot water. After you get used to it, it ain't so hot.

—Minnie Pearl

Wisdom From The Walls

Bathroom Graffiti from around the world

Silence is golden but duct tape is silver.

— • —

On the inside of a toilet door: Patrons are requested to remain seated throughout the entire performance.

— • —

Scrawled under a sign that said "Employees Must Wash Hands":
I waited and waited, but I finally washed them myself.

— • —

Just when I was getting used to yesterday, along came today.

— • —

Roses are Blue
Violets are Pink
Your HDTV
Is on the blink.

— • —

Beauty is in the eye of the beer holder.

If one synchronized swimmer drowns, do all the rest have to drown too?
—Steven Wright

Seen on the bathroom wall of Concordia University:
'Ignorance is bliss.' -and, right underneath it-
'I don't know what this means but I'm happy.'

— • —

Save the whales!
Redeem them later for valuable prizes.

— • —

Support bacteria - they're the only culture some people have.

— • —

Written on a freshly painted bathroom stall: Sometimes a blank
wall is more eloquent than anything that might besmirch it.

— • —

Oscar is Wilde but Thornton is Wilder.

— • —

You may be witty but John Greenleaf is Whittier.

— • —

Confucius say: Man who stand on toilet is high on pot.

My uncle's funeral cost five thousand dollars so far.
We buried him in a rented tuxedo.
—Dave Madden

Fourth Law of Thermodynamics: Anything dropped in
the bathroom invariably goes in the toilet.

— • —

Celibacy is not hereditary.

— • —

Make crime pay- become a lawyer.

— • —

Make love, not war. Heck, do both - get married!

— • —

If life is a waste of time, and time is a waste of life, then let's all get
wasted and have the time of our lives.

— • —

The Eleventh Commandment: Thou shall not commit adulthood.

— • —

To do is to be. (Descartes)
To be is to do. (Voltaire)
Do be do be do. (Sinatra)

I called a discount exterminator.
A guy came by with a rolled-up magazine.
—Will Shriner

More Pretty Good Jokes

This fellow walks by an optometrist's shop. Displayed in the storefront window is a gigantic pair of sunglasses accompanied by a sign, "Nudie Sunglasses!" The chap is intrigued, goes inside and asks the optometrist about them. The optometrist says, "Try them on and see for yourself."

The guy tries on the giant sunglasses, looks at the optometrist and can't believe what he sees. The optometrist appears totally naked! "Does this mean that when I put on these sunglasses everyone becomes nude?"

"That's right."

Well, the guy just has to have them, so he buys a pair and heads home. When he gets there, he opens the door, puts on his new nudie sunglasses and walks into the living room. There he sees his wife sitting on the couch with his neighbor, both appearing to be stark naked. "You're not going to believe this, Dear," says the guy, "but I just bought these super duper sunglasses."

He takes them off to show her and notices the wife and neighbor are still nude.

"Geez," he complains, "I've only had these sunglasses half an hour and they're broken already!"

Ants can carry twenty times their own body weight, which is useful information if you're moving out and you need help getting a potato chip across town.
—**Ron Darian**

Thelma's bathtub was leaking so she called the plumber and made arrangements for him to come the next day. She told the plumber, "I'll be at work, so I'll leave a key under the mat. Oh, and don't worry about my dog, Killer. He won't bother you, but whatever you do, don't talk to my parrot. I can't stress this enough- Do Not Talk To My Parrot!!!"

The next day when the plumber arrived at Thelma's place, he saw the biggest, meanest-looking dog he'd ever seen in his life. But, as Thelma said, Killer just relaxed on the carpet outside the bathroom, watching the plumber as he fixed the tub.

The parrot, on the other hand, was a complete nuisance and drove the plumber crazy with his non-stop cursing, yelling and name calling. At one point, the plumber couldn't take it any longer and yelled, "Shut up you stupid, ugly excuse for a bird!"

The parrot replied, "Get him, Killer!"

•

One snowy morning a husband and wife wake up and hear the latest forecast on the radio. "Five to six inches more of the white stuff is expected. Alternate side of the street parking is in effect. You can only park on the even numbered side of the street today, folks." With that, the wife gets dressed, goes out and moves her car to the other side of the street.

The other day I bought a wastebasket and carried it home in a paper bag. And when I got home, I put the paper bag in the wastebasket.
—**Lily Tomlin**

A week later she hears a similar forecast. "Three to six inches expected this morning. Parking on only the odd numbered side of the street today."

The wife goes out and moves the car again.

A few days later, comes this radio announcement: "We're going to be hit with a big snowstorm today. As far as parking goes…"

All of the sudden, the power is lost! The worried wife turns to her husband and says, "Now I don't know where to park my car. What should I do?"

The husband answers, "I'd say you should just leave it in the garage."

•

A guy goes to see an investment banker who's extremely impressed with the fellow's portfolio and says, "I see you've made a considerable fortune over the years. How so?"

The guy says, "I made it all in the carrier pigeon business."

"Carrier pigeons? Wow! How many could you possibly have sold?"

"Only one, but he kept coming back."

They say the dog is man's best friend. I don't believe that. How many of your friends have you neutered?
—Larry Reeb

A couple gets married and has a baby. But the marriage is a rocky one, and two years into it, they separate. However, as they say, love conquers all and they decide to live together again.

Everything is going swimmingly so the woman asks the fellow to marry her again.

"That's crazy!" exclaims the guy. "You expect me to marry a woman with a kid?!"

•

A guy staggers out of a bar and realizes he's in no shape to drive. He leaves his car in the parking lot and starts to walk home. As he's stumbling along, a cop stops him.

"What's up buddy?"

"I'm goin' to a lecture," slurs the guy.

"At two in the morning? Just who is giving a lecture at this hour?" the cop suspiciously asks.

"My wife."

THOUGHTS OF THE THRONE

I like to buy a four-pack of toilet paper every time I shop, just so I can ask the clerk this judgment question: 'Would you say I got the right amount of toilet paper for the amount of groceries I bought?'

—Pat Hazell

Two groups of doctors and lawyers were heading to their respective conventions by train. The doctors all had tickets but the lawyers had bought only one between them. Having no love for lawyers, the doctors thought this very odd and shared some good laughs over it, expecting the lawyers to get thrown off the train. As the conductor came down the aisle, the lawyers all piled in the bathroom. The conductor knocked on the door and said, "Ticket please," and one ticket slid under the door.

The doctors were annoyed to see lawyers get away with this, so on their way back, they resolved to buy only one ticket and try the same trick as the lawyers. The lawyers one-upped them yet again by not buying any tickets at all. The doctors couldn't see how the lawyers could possibly get away with that.

When the conductor started down the aisle, the lawyers all ran for the bathroom. The doctors all piled in the other bathroom. That's when one of the lawyers came out, knocked on the doctors' bathroom and said, "Ticket please."

•

Long, long ago there was a young Indian lad named Falling Rock. One day he wandered off from the reservation. His parents were very concerned and looked for him everywhere, but days and weeks went by with no sign of him. They mounted a huge publicity cam-

> *My favorite health club is the International House of Pancakes. Because no matter what you weigh, there will always be someone who weighs 150 pounds more than you.*
> **—Lewis Black**

paign to help find him. Signs were put up everywhere in the attempt to locate the youngster. Alas, the lad has yet to be found. But their hope remains that somewhere, someday he will be located. And that is why, to this day, you may be driving down a roadside and be reminded to "Watch for Falling Rock."

•

A drop-dead, gorgeous model is about to undergo a minor procedure and is lying on a gurney in the hospital hallway while waiting for her doctor. A guy in a white coat comes up to her, lifts up the sheet covering her, and visually examines her naked body. He motions to another man in a white coat who then approaches the stunning model and performs the same exam. When a third guy in a white coat approaches, the model asks, "These examinations are okay, I suppose, but when are you going to start the operation?"

The first guy stares blankly and says, "Your guess is as good as ours. We're just here to paint the walls."

•

Roy and Harry are out walking on a Florida nature trail. All of the sudden, Roy says, "Wow, did you see that?"

Harry says, "No."

"Well," says Roy, pointing at a lake, "A crocodile was sunning

The Second Amendment gave us the right to bear arms in order to have a ready militia. It's not for traffic incidents.
—Paula Poundstone

himself on a rock over there and just splashed into the water."

"Hmmm."

A few moments later Roy says, "Did you see that?"

Harry replies, "See what?"

"Are you blind, Harry? A bald eagle just flew overhead."

"Oh."

A few minutes later, Roy says, "Did you see that?"

By this time, Harry is getting a bit exasperated so he says, "As a matter of fact, I did."

"Well then, why did you step in it?"

•

Frank was sitting in a men's room stall minding his own business when a guy occupied the next stall over.

All of a sudden Frank heard, "Hello, how are you doing?"

"Er, ah, well, okay I guess," said Frank, who was not used to carrying on conversations with strangers in public bathrooms.

"How long are you planning to stay?"

According to a survey, eighty-five percent of men admit they surf the Internet wearing nothing but their underwear. Sixty-three percent said that's how they lost their job.

—Jay Leno

"Geez, a couple more minutes I guess," Frank stammered in response.

"Having any problems?" the voice asked.

"Certainly not!" responded Frank, a bit indignantly.

Then the other fellow said, "Look, Charlie I'll call you back. Whenever I say anything, the idiot in the next stall keeps answering me."

•

A guy was sitting in jail talking to his buddy on a phone.
"Man! Reception is lousy," said his pal. "How many bars do you have in your cell?"

• • •

Q&A

Q: What do you call a stupid entry on Twitter?
A: A Nit-Twit.

•

Q: What do you get when you cross an elephant with a kangaroo?
A: Holes all over Australia.

┌─ THOUGHTS OF THE THRONE ─

Q: *How many men does it take to put down a toilet seat?*

A: *Who knows - it's never been done.*

Q: What do you get when you cross a lawyer with a snake?
A: Incest.

•

Q: What would you get if you crossed a cockroach with a lawyer?
A: Nothing. Even cockroaches have some standards.

•

Q: What is the technical meteorological term for a warm, sunny
day that follows two cold, rainy days?
A: Monday.

•

Q: What's the penalty for bigamy?
A: Two mothers-in-law.

•

Q: What did one flea say to the other when they came out of the theater?
A: "Shall we walk or take the dog?"

•

Q: Why can't LeBron James make change for a dollar?
A: Because he's only good for three quarters.

---

*Last night I dreamt I had insomnia. When I woke up I was completely
exhausted but too well rested to go back to sleep.*
—**Bob Nickman**

Q: Why did the Pilgrims' pants always fall down?
A: Because they wore their belt buckles on their hats.

•

Q: Why did the chicken cross the Internet?
A: To get to the other site.

•

Q: How do mermaids keep in contact?
A: With shell phones.

•

Q: Why do mermaids wear seashells?
A: Because B-shells are too small and D-shells are too big.

•

Q: How do you telephone a police dog?
A: Dial K911.

•

Q: Why are computers like women?
A: Because as soon as you have one, you start spending all your money on upkeep and maintenance and no one understands how they think.

You know you're getting old when you're more attractive upside down.
—Cathy Ladman

Ad-Nauseum

Electrolux's ad slogan translated in Scandanavian became, "Nothing sucks like an Electrolux."

•

It wasn't until sometime after GM introduced its prized new auto in Latin America that it found out its name, Nova, when translated means, "It won't go."

•

Jolly Green Giant in Arabic is "Intimidating Green Ogre."

•

In Chinese, the Kentucky Fried Chicken slogan "Finger Lickin' Good" means "Eat your fingers off."

•

Hunt-Wesson introduced its Big John products in French Canada as "Gros Jos" only to find out that the phrase, in slang, means "big breasts."

•

"Got Milk?" in Spanish is "Are you lactating?"

•

Coors "Turn it Loose" campaign in Spanish: "Suffers from diarrhea."

All those animal rights people get on my nerves. They don't want to save all the animals, they just want to save the cute ones. You'll never see a 'Save the Lab Rat' campaign.
—**Drew Carey**

Great Moments in Foresight

Decca Recording Company, rejecting a new English band in 1962: "We don't like their sound, and guitar music is on the way out." Yup. It was The Beatles.

•

Charles Duell, commissioner of the U.S. Office of Patents, in 1899: "Everything that can be invented has been invented."

•

Thomas Watson, IBM chairman, evaluating the business potential of a new contraption in 1943: "I think there is a world market for maybe five computers."

•

"Computers are useless. They can only give you answers." –Pablo Picasso

•

"Video won't be able to hold onto any market it captures after the first six months. People will soon get tired of staring at a plywood box every night." –Darryl F. Zanuck, boss man of 20th Century Fox, about television, 1946

I used to think that the human brain was the most fascinating part of the body. Then I realized, well, look what's telling me that.
—Emo Philips

"The horse is there to stay, but the automobile is only a novelty- a fad." -President of the Michigan Savings Bank, telling Henry Ford's lawyer not to invest in the Ford Motor Company, 1903

•

"You ain't going nowhere, son. You ought to go back to drivin' a truck." -Manager of the Grand Ole Opry, dismissing Elvis Presley after just one performance

•

"I don't think you're going to see a great, great uproar in this country about the Republican committee trying to bug the Democratic headquarters." -President Richard Nixon, just after the Watergate break-in

•

"Man will never reach the moon, regardless of all future scientific advances." -Dr. Lee DeForest, Inventor, 1957

•

"God himself could not sink this ship." -Titanic deckhand, Southampton, England, April 10, 1912

*My husband thinks that health food is anything he eats
before the expiration date.*
—Rita Rudner

Criminally Stupid

We all have sympathy for people who are none too bright. After all, we have moments of cluelessness ourselves from time to time. But when people use their minimal mental powers to victimize others and it backfires, we can all treat ourselves to a good hearty laugh.

A North Carolina woman went into the local bank with a check made out to the Tension Envelope Company. In trying to cash it she claimed to be Mrs. Tension Envelope. The teller wasn't buying it. This was one Envelope that definitely wasn't going anywhere. The bank put in a call to the police who quickly changed her name from Mrs. Envelope to Mrs. Case File.

•

A gang tried to break into a fireworks factory with a cutting torch. They were almost through the door when the flame ignited a case of fireworks sitting nearby. It had the explosive force of a hundred pounds of gunpowder and triggered the explosion of the entire factory, which went up in a spectacular mushroom cloud. Their cutting equipment was scattered around and their getaway car was crushed when a section of the roof landed on it. Unfortunately, the crooks were never located and apparently got away. To this day the police refer to them as "The Hole in the Ground Gang".

> *My father hugged me only once, on my twenty-first birthday. It was very awkward. I now know what it was that made me feel so uncomfortable: the nudity.*
> **—Ray Romano**

A bank robber in Manchester, New Hampshire, thought dressing up as a tree was the perfect disguise. He duct-taped branches to his head and body and leaves to his face, then went in for the stick up. Fortunately, the security camera didn't have the old problem of not being able to see the forest for the trees and got enough shots of his face for police to root him out. Whether he was a shady character or a tree-time loser, he took the fall and they probably won't spring him for a long, long time.

•

A knife-wielding thug was dissatisfied with the money from the cash register so he looked around for something else to steal. Grabbing a pair of hiking boots, he made his getaway. Days later, the clerk had ID'd the crook and he was arrested. When the trial came up, the DA had a thin case. The only piece of evidence was the positive ID. Feeling confident, the crook leaned back and put his feet up. The judge couldn't believe the crook's stupidity. He was wearing the very boots that had been reported stolen and he was hauled off to the pokey in stocking feet.

•

In Union City, California, a burglar was busy robbing a house when the owner came home. Startled, he ran out of the house, jumped a fence and landed in the neighbor's yard. It so happens, for

You know the problem with men? After the birth, we're irrelevant.
—Dustin Hoffman

reasons he did not bare, he was stark naked. And it so happens that when he jumped the fence he landed in the neighbor's prize cactus. Hey, like they say, don't do the crime if you can't do the spines.

•

They say a criminal always returns to the scene of the crime, but not usually for this reason. A burglar had gotten away scot-free with the TV. The mistake he made that led to his arrest was coming back a few hours later to steal the remote.

•

Portsmouth, Rhode Island, police figured they had the right guy when they arrested a man for a string of vending machine robberies. By the time he posted his $400 bond they felt even more confident. It was completely in coins.

•

He had seen all the cop shows. Most of the movies, too. He knew when you held somebody up you needed to cover your face. So he did. With a bag. A plastic bag. The police had an excellent description- besides, he was way too out-of-breath to run very far.

THOUGHTS OF THE THRONE

I found out why cats drink out of the toilet. My mother told me it's because the water is cold in there. And I'm like, how did my mother know that?

—Wendy Liebman

Canada is a kinder, gentler land. In Ontario, a shopkeeper was held up by a man armed with toilet bowl cleaner. He didn't get far. The police caught him blue-handed.

•

In Georgia, a forty-one year-old man held up a gas station with his face partially covered. That might have worked with someone else, but the attendant on duty at the time was his daughter.

•

The prosecutor wheeled around and placed his hands on the witness stand.

"You say you were robbed of your purse by two men while walking down the street?"

"Yes sir," the witness meekly responded.

"And do you see the men in this courtroom today?" he pressed dramatically.

Before the witness could answer, the two defendants raised their hands and nodded as if to signal that they were present. At this point Perry Mason couldn't have gotten them off- not that he could have been heard over the laughter of the judge and jury.

I told my psychiatrist I have suicidal tendencies.
He told me to pay in advance.
—Rodney Dangerfield

The motel clerk and all those who were in the lobby were momentarily struck by horror when Karen Lee Joachimi burst in and attempted to hold up the place with a chainsaw. They no doubt flashed back to all those gruesome horror movies. Fortunately, they then flashed forward to "Funniest Home Videos" when they realized that the chainsaw was electric and Karen had neglected to plug it in!

•

A New Jersey high school student felt that a snowstorm would be a good time to rob his local 7-11. He came up to the clerk, pulled a gun and made off with $50. He didn't get a chance to spend it though- the police merely followed his footprints from the store all the way to his front door.

•

Two bored British teens decided to break into a grocery store but bit off more than they could chew. The inexperienced duo spotted what they thought was the cash box on the wall. They pried it off and ran for it. The box began buzzing and howling during their getaway so they threw it to the ground and stomped on it in an effort to shut the thing up.

But the box just kept getting louder and louder as they ran. In desperation, they finally tossed it in the river. It turns out the pimply-faced perpetrators stole the store's burglar alarm instead of the cash box.

Do you like historical facts? President Lincoln wore a stovepipe hat. The guy that sat behind him at Ford's Theatre only saw the second half of the show.
—David Letterman

Signs Of The Times

Golf Balls the Size of Hail
-in front of a Fairhope, Alabama, golf shop

— • —

PULL. If that doesn't work, PUSH. If that doesn't work, we're closed. Come again.
-on the post office door in Esperance, New York

— • —

You Don't Have to Sleep With That Drip Tonight.
-on a plumber's truck in Pittsburgh

— • —

Open seven days a week and weekends.
-in a New Jersey restaurant

— • —

Mental Health Prevention Center
-in a New York medical building

— • —

Do not activate with wet hands.
-on a restroom dryer at Chicago's O'Hare Field

What's the shelf life of a shelf?
—Jason Love

Medicine Through The Ages

2000 B.C. - Here, eat this root.
1000 A.D. - That root is heathen. Here, say this prayer.
1850 A.D. - That prayer is superstition. Here, drink this potion.
1940 A.D. - That potion is snake oil. Here, swallow this pill.
1985 A.D. - That pill is ineffective. Here, take this antibiotic.
2000 A.D. - That antibiotic is artificial. Here, eat this root.

• • •

Food For Thought

Is it true that cannibals won't eat clowns because they taste funny?

•

Q: If a cannibal ate his mother's sister, what would you call him?
A: An aunt-eater.

•

Noticing the down in the mouth look on his friend's face, the cannibal said to his buddy, "What's the matter? Your wife makes a good stew."

"I know, but now who am I going to play cards with?"

A new computer virus is going around. Office workers everywhere will now be forced to play solitaire with real cards.
—Craig Kilborn

Two cannibals were scavenging through a garbage can. One of them came across a discarded "Sports Illustrated" swimsuit issue and said to the other, "Look at this menu!"

•

One cannibal says to the other, "You know, I really don't care for my mother-in-law."

"Just eat your vegetables then."

•

Q: What are cannibals' favorite cookies?
A: Girl Scouts.

•

Two cannibals were out hiking early one morning when they came upon two campers in sleeping bags.

"Look," said one cannibal to the other, "breakfast in bed!"

•

Two cannibals went to their favorite restaurant. "Look," said one, "there's a politician on the menu tonight."

"Sweet," said the other. "I love baloney sandwiches."

I had my car towed. There's nothing wrong with it.
That was just cheaper than buying a tank of gas.
—Jay Leno

Bathroom Briefs #2

Not Too Sharp
Back in 1902, Gillette started selling safety razors, but hundreds of men threw them away in frustration. Just like guys today, they never bothered to read the instructions. You had to unwrap the razors first!

•

Flipping His Lid
A diner at a Stockholm, Sweden, restaurant walked into the men's room and discovered all the seats were gone. While reporting this to the manager, he spotted all the seats being loaded into the dishwasher along with the dishes. The manager claimed that this would make them toasty and warm to sit on but this customer wasn't taking it sitting down and called in the health inspector.

•

Bathroom Ballistics
There are all sorts of things to fear in a public rest room- germs, running out of paper, cold seats- but a 53 year-old Tampa woman discovered yet another: getting shot. As she was using the ladies room in a local hotel, the woman in the next stall dropped a gun from her waist holster and upon hitting the floor, it went off.

Without question, the greatest invention in the history of mankind is beer. Oh, I grant you that the wheel was also a fine invention, but the wheel does not go nearly as well with pizza.
—Dave Barry

Fortunately, the bullet hit the victim in the lower leg and her injury was relatively minor. And you think you've had unpleasant things emanate from the next stall.

•

Toilet Bowl Ring

A Phoenix plumber was deep into the glop and the goo but he came up with the prize- a $70,000 diamond ring flushed down the toilet at a diner. The seven carat jewel is now known as "The Diamond in the Roughage".

•

Rear End Collision

A San Antonio woman probably wished she had a seatbelt on her commode when a car crashed into her home at a high speed and threw her off her porcelain perch. She wasn't injured but the Tydee Bowl man was knocked overboard and has never been seen again.

•

Foul Territory

What's worse than having your gold tooth fall into a toilet at Citi Field during a Mets game? Going in after it and having your arm stuck for hours as the high vacuum system continuously tries to

*Somebody said to me, "But The Beatles were antimaterialistic."
That is a huge myth. John and I literally used to sit down and say,
"Now, let's write a swimming pool."*
—Paul McCartney

flush you. A female Mets fan got into just that predicament, doing about as well in the john as the Mets were on the field. The plumber who installed the system had to be located and he finally managed to extract her after several hours of being flushed up to her armpit. She lost her tooth and the Mets lost the game- so ends the story in Flushing, New York.

•

Rantin' in Scranton

An off-duty police officer in Scranton, Pennsylvania, heard his neighbor swearing at her toilet though an open window. It seemed her throne wouldn't flush and she was expressing her displeasure. Imagine how she felt when he arrested her and took her downtown to introduce her to the municipal facilities. The ACLU took the cop to court and the judge ruled that her latrine language was constitutionally protected free speech and that the city owed the woman $28,000 dollars- more than enough to cover the plumbing bill.

•

NEWS FLUSH! Suicidal Twin Kills Sister By Mistake

THOUGHTS OF THE THRONE

What do you get on Mother's Day if you have kids?
A card with flowers that are made out of pink toilet paper –
a lot of pink toilet paper. You get breakfast in bed. Then you
get up and fix everybody else their breakfast. And then you
go to the bathroom, and you are out of toilet paper.

—Liz Scott

Quote, Unquote

Your job is to complete the following quote by filling in the missing word. Its correlating letters can be obtained from the stage names of the funny people whose real names are listed below.

"If you don't want your dog to have bad breath, do what I do: Pour a little Lavoris in the _ _ _ _ _ _." –Jay Leno

1. _ _ _ _ _ _ (1) _ _ _
   Birth name: Scott Thompson

2. _ (2) _ _   _ _ _ _ _ _ _
   Birth name: Joan Molinsky

3. _ (3) _ _ _ _
   Birth name: David Adkins

4. _ _ _ _ _ _ _   _ _ (4) _ _ _ _ _
   Birth name: Caryn Johnson

5. _ _ _ (5) _   _ _ _ _ _
   Birth name: Eric Bishop

6. _ _ _ _ _   (6) _ _   _ _ _ _ _ _   _ _ _
   Birth name: Daniel Whitney

___ ___ ___ ___ ___ ___
 1   2   3   4   5   6

Interest your kids in bowling. Get them off the streets and into the alleys.
—Don Rickles

Answers:

1. Scott Thompson- Carrot Top
2. Joan Molinsky- Joan Rivers
3. David Adkins- Sinbad
4. Caryn Johnson- Whoopi Goldberg
5. Eric Bishop- Jamie Foxx
6. Daniel Whitney- Larry the Cable Guy

"If you don't want your dog to have bad breath, do what I do: Pour a little Lavoris in the t o i l e t." –Jay Leno

• • •

5 Apt Anagrams

Dormitory	Dirty Room
Election Results	Lies- Let's Recount
Snooze Alarms	Alas! No More Zs
Slot Machines	Cash Lost in 'em
Mother-In-Law	Woman Hitler

THOUGHTS OF THE THRONE

When I was in elementary school we signed each other's yearbooks and I would often write: May your life be like a roll of toilet paper, long and useful.

—Jennifer Lutz

Blunders and Boo-Boos

In Clermont, France, a man had a stubborn grease stain on his shirt so he went to that old and very dangerous standby- gasoline. He poured about a cup of the stuff in the washer and hoped for the best. What he got was the worst. When the washer changed cycles, a tiny spark ignited the gas and the first floor of his home pretty much disappeared. The man was knocked unconscious. When he woke up his only comment was, "I feel pretty stupid." At least the gasoline lived up to the universal claim of detergents everywhere. It indeed made everything as fresh as the outdoors.

•

An Arizona man, imagining himself King of the Wild Frontier, set out for some hunting and bagged his limit- of legs. First he accidentally shot himself in the leg and then he got the bright idea to fire his rifle to signal for help. That's when he shot himself in the other leg.

•

Everyone has had bad days but one young laboratory worker set the bar pretty high. While going about his duties, he noticed a wasp's nest in the facility and determined that a vacuum cleaner would be the best tool to get rid of the pests. It was only after he sucked them up that he realized he could not switch off the vacuum or they'd

I'm really bad with names. Yesterday I saw a guy choking, and performed the Kevorkian maneuver on him.
—**Craig Sharf**

escape. He went and got a can of bug spray and emptied the entire spray can down the vacuum hose. What he hadn't realized was that bug spray in aerosol form is explosive. The vacuum motor's brushes threw out tiny sparks. The explosion burnt off his eyebrows and threw him to the floor where he regained his senses only after the other survivors of the blast showed up to express their displeasure. He suffered burns, minor injuries and many, many stings but he learned several valuable lessons that day including, "let sleeping wasps lie".

•

An Oklahoma woman purchased a 32-foot motor home, drove it onto the freeway, set the cruise control for 70 mph and then got up and went in the back to make a sandwich. A few seconds later, she crashed. She sued the manufacturer for $1,750,000, claiming that nowhere in the manual did it advise against doing this. She won the full amount plus a new motor home.

THOUGHTS OF THE THRONE

Making coffee has become the great compromise of the decade. It's the only thing "real" men do that doesn't seem to threaten their masculinity. To women, it's on the same domestic entry level as putting the spring back into the toilet-tissue holder or taking a chicken out of the freezer to thaw.

—**Erma Bombeck**

Things You Don't Want To Hear From Technical Support

"Do you have a sledgehammer or a brick handy?"

— • —

"Press 1 for Support. Press 2 if you're with '60 Minutes'. Press 3 if you're with the FTC."

— • —

"We can fix this, but you'll need a Swiss knife, a roll of duct tape, and a car battery."

— • —

"You ought to get a new computer. The prices are their lowest in years."

— • —

"Looks like you're gonna need some new dilythium crystals, Cap'n."

— • —

"Bummer, Dude."

— • —

"Please hold for Mr. Gates' lawyer."

People want to know why I do this, why I write such gross stuff.
I like to tell them I have the heart of a small boy and I
keep it in a jar on my desk.
—Stephen King

Resume Rejects

Actual items gleaned from resumes of people who are probably still looking for work.

"Wholly responsible for two failed financial institutions."

•

"It's best for employers that I not work with people."

•

"The company made me a scapegoat, just like my three previous employers."

•

"My goal is to be a meteorologist. But since I possess no training in meteorology, I suppose I should try stock brokerage."

•

"I have an excellent track record, although I am not a horse."

THOUGHTS OF THE THRONE

Q: *What happened to the Native American who drank too much tea?*

A: *He drowned in his own tea pee.*

Bytes of Humor

Q: Where do computers go on vacation?
A: To the Big Apple

•

Q: What's the best way to park a computer?
A: You back it up.

•

Q: What did the football punter do to the computer?
A: He booted it up.

•

Q: What happens when you cross a computer with an elephant?
A: I don't know but you get plenty of memory.

•

Q: What is an astronaut's favorite key on a computer keyboard?
A: The space bar

•

Q: What happened when the computer fell on the floor?
A: It slipped a disk.

•

Q: Why was there a bug in the computer?
A: It was looking for a byte to eat.

Blessed are the young, for they shall inherit the national debt.
—Herbert Hoover

You Know E-Mail Has Become Way Too Important When...

You sneer derisively at people with only a 56K Internet connection.

•

You start using Smileys in your snail mail.

•

You refer to going to the bathroom as downloading.

•

All of your friends have an @ in their names.

•

You start tilting your head sideways to smile.

•

When told you have no new mail, you refuse to believe it and check it again.

Thoughts of the Throne

European toilet paper is made from the same material that Americans use for roofing, which is why Europeans tend to remain standing throughout soccer matches.

—**Dave Barry**

Man's Wisdom of the Ages

At birth, you know nothing.

At 10, you know enough to know you want to know a lot more.

At 20, you think you know everything.

At 30, you know you know everything, and don't want to know any more.

40- Know too much

50- Know you are old enough to know better

60- Know you wish you'd known then what you know now

70- Forgetting everything you ever knew yet want no knowledge of anything new

80- Know what's worth knowing

90- Know you really never knew anything but find comfort in who you've known

100- Know that if you didn't wise up by 90, you're ready for the Great Unknown

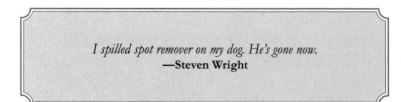

I spilled spot remover on my dog. He's gone now.
—**Steven Wright**

From The Classifieds

Wanted: Human cannonball – must be able to travel

•

Amana washer $100. Owned by clean bachelor who seldom washed.

•

Tired of working for only $9.75 per hour? We offer profit-sharing and flexible hours. Starting pay, $7-9 per hour.

•

Girl wanted to assist magician in cutting-off-head illusion. Blue Cross and salary.

•

Snow blower for sale...only used on snowy days.

•

Free puppies...part German Shepherd, part dog

•

1 man, 7 woman hot tub — $850/offer

I am not a vegetarian because I love animals;
I am a vegetarian because I hate plants.
—A. Whitney Brown

Addled Ads

Stock up and save. Limit: one.

•

Our bikinis are exciting. They are simply the tops.

•

Whirlpool built-in oven—frost-free.

•

Hummels—largest selection ever. If it's in stock, we have it!

•

We do not tear your clothing with machinery. We do it carefully by hand.

•

Illiterate? Write today for free help.

•

Auto Repair Service. Free pick-up and delivery. Try us once, you'll never go anywhere again.

•

Used cars—why go elsewhere to be cheated? Come here first!

THOUGHTS OF THE THRONE

You know you're getting fat when you sit in your bathtub and the water in the toilet rises.

—**Etta May**

Even More Pretty Good Jokes

A guy walks into a tavern and says to the bartender, "I'll have three shots, one for both of my friends and one for me."

This goes on for a few weeks until, one day, he orders only two drinks. The bartender quizzically asks, "What happened, did one of our friends die?"

"No, I stopped drinking."

•

A young man wanted to get his beautiful wife something nice for their first wedding anniversary. So he decided to buy her a hot new cell phone-one with all the features.

The next day, the wife was shopping and the phone rang. It was her husband testing out the phone.

"Hi Honey," he says. "How do you like your new phone?"

"I just love it, it's so nice to be able to call any time, anywhere. It's so handy with the time and calculator and games and everything but there's one thing I don't understand."

"What's that, baby?" asked the husband.

"How did you know to call me at the mall?"

My father told me all about the birds and the bees.
The liar- I went steady with a woodpecker till I was twenty-one.
—Bob Hope

With the economy tightening, the husband and wife sat down at the kitchen table to figure how to make ends meet.

"Well the first thing that should go is your beer," the wife stated flatly. "At $30 a case, it's just too rich for our blood."

"That's all well and good," the husband replied. "But what about that $75 you spent on makeup last week?"

"That was to make me look beautiful for you," she retorted, a bit wounded.

"That's crazy," he snapped. "What do you think the beer was for?"

•

During a visit to a mental asylum, a visitor asked the psychiatrist what criterion defined whether a person was crazy or not.

"Well," said the psychiatrist, "we fill up a bathtub; then we give the patient a choice of a teaspoon, a soup ladle, and a bucket and ask him or her to empty the bathtub."

"Oh, I get it," said the visitor. "A normal person would use the bucket because it's bigger than the spoon or the ladle."

"No," said the psychiatrist, "A normal person would pull the plug."

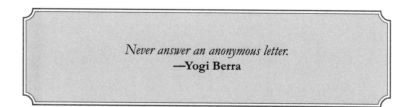

Never answer an anonymous letter.
—Yogi Berra

A husband and wife were at a fancy restaurant when the husband noticed that his better half kept glancing at a drunk a few tables away.

"That's terrible- look at him, drunk as a skunk," she hissed.

"Do you know him?" the husband inquired.

"I certainly do," the wife shot back. "That's my ex-husband and he's been drinking like that since I left him ten years ago."

"Wow!" exclaimed the husband. "I didn't know anybody could celebrate that long."

•

A guy was shopping for dinner at a supermarket when a beautiful redhead smiled and waved at him. He couldn't figure out where he knew her from but nonetheless he was thrilled at the attention until she walked up and said, "I think you're the father of one of my kids."

Taken aback, he initially denied it but then he searched his memory. "Wait a minute," he blurted out. "That night my buddies got me drunk and took all my clothes and set me out on Main Street and I wandered around until I came into this little bar and fell in the mud-wrestling pit and vomited all over the floor... Were you the stripper who took me home with her that night?"

"No," she answered coolly. "I'm your son's math teacher."

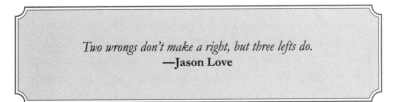

Two wrongs don't make a right, but three lefts do.
—Jason Love

A Priest and a Rabbi were relaxing at the town's Fourth of July picnic when the Priest got the urge to have a little fun.

"I'll tell you Rabbi, you just haven't lived until you've tried Mrs. Bellcourt's prized Virginia Baked Ham. Do you think you might break down and give it a go?"

"Probably," the Rabbi answered with a faint smile. "At your wedding."

•

A man driving an enormous motor home got hopelessly bogged down in an unexpected muddy hole along a dirt road on the way to a popular campground. As luck would have it after only a few minutes, a passing farmer drove by on his tractor and offered to pull him out for only $20.

After the motor home was back on dry ground the grateful man said to the farmer, "At those prices, I bet you're pulling RVs out of this mud day and night."

"All day maybe," replied the farmer. "At night I haul water for the hole."

•

Q: What did the 0 say to the 8?
A: Nice belt!

When you're a dad you can't keep your cool car. Fancy stereo, power windows, sunroof; the kids are going to kill all that stuff. Take an ordinary cookie. In the hands of a kid it becomes a sugar hand grenade. You have to take the car into the shop because chocolate chips are clogging the carburetor.
—Sinbad

Gina, a very well put together secretary from New Jersey, went on vacation in California. The first day, she went up to the roof of her hotel to get in a little sunbathing so she grabbed her book and began soaking up the sun's rays. The next day she thought that since no one could see her, she'd go for an all-over tan. She had hardly laid down when she heard footsteps coming up the stairs. Since she was lying on her stomach, she just pulled a towel over her bottom.

"Ma'am, we really don't mind you sunbathing up here but we must ask that you wear a bathing suit as you did yesterday," the manager gasped out between breaths.

"I don't see why," Gina replied. "I'm high enough here that no one can see me. Besides, I'm covered with a towel."

"Not exactly," the manager said. "You're lying on the dining room skylight."

•

Farmer Ziffle was having trouble with some local rascals who snuck into his watermelon patch every night to eat their fill. After pondering the problem for a while, he had an inspiration. He painted a sign that said, "WARNING! One of the watermelons in this patch has been injected with rat poison!"

Yesterday I was a dog. Today I'm a dog. Tomorrow I'll probably still be a dog. Sigh! There's so little hope for advancement.
—Snoopy

The next night he hid nearby to watch what would happen and sure enough, the kids read the sign and ran for home. Ziffle was still feeling self-satisfied a few days later when he came out to survey the field, but once he got there, he turned pale. No watermelons were missing but a sign had been added just below his:

"Now there are two!"

• • •

A Few Good Lawyer Jokes

What's the difference between an onion and a lawyer?
When you cut the onion, you cry.

•

Who invented copper wire?
Two tax lawyers fighting over a penny.

•

What's the definition of a lawyer?
Someone who makes sure he gets what's coming to you.

•

What's black and brown and looks good on a lawyer?
A Doberman.

Do you know the real reason Lincoln was shot in the theater?
His cell phone kept going off.
—Jay Leno

Pranks For The Privy

Our lavatorial staff is flushed with excitement to present some easy, effective practical jokes for a transformation of outhouse to funhouse.

Give your toilet some pop by taping plastic bubble wrap on the underside of the lid and then gently put down the seat to await your victim.

•

Take the shower head off and place a bouillon cube inside it. Be prepared. The victim is sure to have a beef afterward.

•

Paint the shower soap with transparent nail polish. Trying to lather up will be no piece of cake.

•

Our "Five-Flush" Favorite! Get a Sharpie marker and two pieces of toilet paper. Write "Help!" backwards (!PLEH) on the toilet paper and place it neatly on the water in the bowl. A while later, the message will still be clearly visible and the paper barely detectable. It's a beautiful thing!

THOUGHTS OF THE THRONE

Why is it that K-Mart won't take back underwear that's been opened, but they'll take back a toilet seat within 30 days?

—**Nick Tarr**

Real Epitaphs- May You R.I.P.*

*Here lies Jane Smith, wife
of Thomas Smith, marble
cutter. This monument was
erected by her husband as a
tribute to her memory and a
specimen of his work.
Monuments of the same
style 350 dollars.*
-Springdale, Ohio

•

*Stranger, approach this
spot with gravity.
John Brown is filling his
last cavity.*
-for a dentist

•

The Cubs Stink!
**-on a Yiddish tombstone,
Chicago, Illinois**

•

This is on me…
-Rhode Island

*In memory of
Mrs. Alpha White
Weight 309 lbs
Open wide ye heavenly gates
That lead to the
heavenly shore;
Our father suffered in
passing through
And mother weighs much more.*
-Lee, Massachusetts

•

*Looked up the elevator shaft
to see if the car was
on the way down.
It was.*
-in Albany, New York

•

*Here lies an atheist
All dressed up
And no place to go.*
-in Thurmond, Maryland

* Read In Potty

---

*Did you ever hear someone say this: "It was more fun than a barrel of
monkeys." Did you ever smell a barrel of monkeys?*
—Steve Bluestein

The World's Shortest Story

He asked
her to marry him.
She said no and he
lived happily ever after,
leaving the toilet seat
up whenever he
felt like it.

The End

THE BATHROOM LIBRARY